I0756588

FINDING BUYERS

How?

Graeme Smith

PUBLISHED ON AMAZON.com
by
LABYRINTH BOOKS

DEDICATION

This book is dedicated to my family.

> **Hele-ly (Ly).**
> > my wife:

> **Ingrid.**
> > our daughter:

> **Marie.**
> > my former wife:

> **Fiona, Natalie and Michael**
> > our children:

> **Georgie**
> > Michael's wife:

> **Pearl, Kiki and Martha.**
> > their children:

They have put up with me for many years and I thank them for that.
> I hope this book gives them an insight into what has occupied me.
> Well for much of the time.
> They have all done worthwhile and interesting things.
> Without much help from me.
> I congratulate them for their achievements.

AN ART CAREER STARTED LIKE THIS.

    1. The nature of art was considered

    2. Related to these aims, are more specific objectives.

    3. That's what SPACE Art Education stands for!

    4. SPACE Art Education makes these assumptions.

1. The nature of art was considered.

    The following are AIMS derived from this analysis.

        To develop the uniqueness of each student.

        To develop confident self-actualization.

        To develop self-responsibility and initiative.

        To develop creativity and flexibility of thinking.

        To develop visual perceptual ability.

    In relation to the individual learner they develop these qualities:

        Unique person

        Self-actualization

        Self-responsibility

        Creativity

        Perceptual skills

    An Art Career assumes creativity is a behaviour all have.

        Even without any teaching.

        Suitable educational methods can develop higher skill levels.

        The value of appropriate behaviour is stressed.

        An interaction of perception, affect and cognition is creativity.

    An Art Career provides appropriate strategies.

        They expose students to the creative process.

        Nurture their creative response.

        And develop creativity skill as a consequence.

        Planned, deliberate, sequenced and non-verbal strategies.

The diagram illustrates the various OBJECTIVES and their relationship to coach strategies and student LEARNING EXPERIENCES.

2. Related to the aims are more specific objectives.

> **Skills attitudes and concepts are integrated and developed.**
> **Thus later stages incorporate earlier ones.**
> **Creativity is the behaviour intrinsic to both art and education.**

STIMULUS Structured	SKILLS Perceptual	ATTITUDES Affective	CONCEPTS Cognitive	LEARNING Experiences
Concrete	Visual Tactual Manipulative	Receiving Responding	Evaluation	Awareness
Sensory		Valuing	Synthesis	Expressive Analysis
Verbal			Organization Application	Experimental Comprehensive
Personal		Value Complex	Knowledge	Existential

3. That's what SPACE Art Education stands for!

> **Structured STIMULUS – a planned and organized program.**
> **Perceptual SKILLS – student develop in response to a stimulus.**
> **Affective ATTITUDES – emotion guides student options.**
> **Cognitive CONCEPTS – creative thinking determines the action.**
> **Experiences LEARNING – which is how learning happens.**

4. Like SPACE Art Education,

> **COACH CREATIVITY SKILL makes these assumptions:**
> 1. The core of creativity is interaction of feeling, thinking and doing.
> 2. Each learning experience should be enjoyable but serious.
> 3. This is primarily a time for student action rather than coach talk.
> 4. The learning experience is seen by the student as self-rewarding

HOW TO USE THIS BOOK.

Usually people don't think through things to the level they need to.
Because of that, they have projects instead of tasks on their "to do" list.
That leads to procrastination for it hasn't been broken down to a task level.
So go through your book once to understand it THEN go through it again.

Then start at the BEGINNING.
Make notes of the steps you will need to take and the resources required.
Use notes to create a step by step system for implementing particular ideas.
Often you won't refer back to an original, once you've created **YOUR** system.

The first question to ask and answer is "Why is this being done?"
How does this align with where you want to get to?
What are the strategic implications of doing this?
Does this fit in with getting to a goal in the shortest and fastest time?
What would it be like if it were totally successful?
Define it - what is success for this project and how will you know?

Now brainstorm all the tasks are involved in your project.
It's important not to go linear too fast with this.
By linear, I mean step one, step two, step three, and step four.
You end up cutting off options.
As you plan step one, two, three, there is a specific step that might be four.
Start steps too quickly, other ways for one, two and three may not appear.

The first third of a brainstorming session is easy - find lots of ideas.
The second third is challenging – look at the ideas to see where they go.
Then push to think a bit outside the box for that's often where the big idea is!
That's where the most powerful way of getting a project done the fastest - is.

Most never get to that level and end up short-changing themselves.
Then their project takes longer and they also set up to procrastinate.
This final brainstorming part of the equation is incredibly important.

Once you've brainstormed a project put options into a linear sequence.
Then you can figure out what you've overlooked and all becomes obvious.
Get tasks in order, add missing steps, and lay out your list for the project.

Once you've organized the tasks into a linear process decide:
What things can you start immediately?
What can start that is not dependent on things that must occur beforehand?
There might be five, six or twenty that don't rely on anything else to happen.
You can get started on them right away!

Write things you think of and cross off things as you do them.
Add in stuff that is relevant from time to time.

MY FOCUS.

I have taken many years to learn lessons and develop materials.
You are welcome to look elsewhere but will not find solutions such as I offer.
Some may even sound similar but they WILL be different.
I doubt if others have the individual components nor philosophical orientation.

ART
What is essential for art to exist?
There **IS** an answer and it is the foundation of An Art Career.
That means this book is grounded in philosophy and so doesn't date.

Whatever art is MUST happen every time art happens!
If Art = x then x must happen whenever art happens.
Not sometimes, occasionally or even mostly BUT - **ALWAYS**.
So what is art?
Art **IS** creativity expressed using visual material.
That is **ALL** art, of any kind, of any standard.
It is an action – something that is done.

CAREER
What values does art have when placed in a commercial context.
All things done in a commercial context are done for business reasons.
Otherwise they are optional.

Is there something about art that can also commercial?
If people pay money there should be some benefit for them.
That should be the focus of an art business program and is of An Art Career.

An Art Career is not rocket science but common sense.
It is art business for the 21st Century brought right up to date in this book.

But it has also been tested in real life.
An Art Career works because it is right.
The thinking and the practice are in harmony.

THE REAL TEST

The success of a professional career is measured by money earned.

Income is the **ONLY** objective way to measure your professional success.

BUT it's not me that will build your art business for you.

You are the professional artist running your business.

To get **ANY** benefit you must actually **DO** something!

There is very little benefit gained by merely reading my material.

INDEX: FINDING BUYERS.

SUPPORT:

The Australian Artist magazine – magazine for artists

Clipping Path Universe – for photo-shop editing

Cherri Computers – computer hardware, software and printers

The International Artist magazine – magazine for artists

1. What is your job?

Reviewed by Eric Spence - (Mississuga, Canada)

1. Your job is to make a living!
2. At the beginning of a career an artist has many things to do.
3. If you know your target market create a hard to refuse offer!
4. Other ways to obtain and use names and addresses.
5. Sorting your names and addresses.
6. As knowledge about prospects grow segment your list.

1. Your job is to make a living!

You probably thought your main job was to paint or teach didn't you?
Yes, you do that, but as a professional artist it is so you can make a living.

Whatever you do you can only make a living if there are clients.
Clients are people who pay money for what you sell.
It might be simple but that isn't the same as saying it's easy.
You can easily spend a lot of money with little to show for it.
But it's not just money you'll spend; time also goes in large doses.
Fortunately retaining the clients you have, has time and money economies.
There is potential for increased sales as well - so it does get easier.

A contact address code is primarily a space saver.
Just a few words, letters and numerals, tell of a person and where they live.

Enter everyone you know to start your contact list.
List your friends, relatives, acquaintances, and so on.
Do not worry about whether they buy your paintings at this stage either.
After all everyone has to start as someone who hasn't bought (yet)!
Just enter them even if details are incomplete.
Enter everybody you do business with.
Your picture framer, galleries, art shows organizers, publishers and others.
After all you never know when you'll need to get in touch, do you?

It is important you choose where you allow your work to be sold.
Collect name, address, email address, phone number before you need them.
Don't forget the electrician, solicitor, accountant, hairdresser, or butcher.
Include all the people who depend on you for some of their income.
So garage mechanic, car dealer, insurance representative, and others.
Also electrician, solicitor, accountant, hairdresser, butcher or gardener.

Real estate agents are a great contact too and are often females.
They meet many who collect art and even advise their clients about things.
When they show property agents consider artwork and its effect on buyers
Just include all the people who depend on you for some of their income.

As before, do not worry about whether they're likely to buy art or not!
In the beginning assume they will, particularly yours.
Don't worry if all the details are there or correct, just enter whatever you can.
As you support these people you can reasonably expect support from them.

Write down everybody you hope to do business with too.
Obviously clients you'd like will be listed.
Anyone you know of who collects, or buys, artworks should be included.
Even include those who might possibly buy artworks.
Many are in the Yellow Pages under 'Medical Practitioner', 'Solicitor', etc.
Check back to the White Pages to find a home address (not all will be there).
No going through magazines, pieces of paper, or letters to contact someone.

Write down other potential contacts for the future.
These are very important people, including spouses and gatekeepers.
Gatekeepers are secretaries, or receptionists for important people.
They determine whether you get to see or talk to the person concerned.
Their co-operation opens doors that would otherwise be hard to penetrate.

If you think you are starting to have a list that is too big, think again.
There is no such thing as a list that's too big, just add the names and details.
Collecting contact information is a standard professional activity.

Once you have started your contact list add to it all the time.
When you read a newspaper add to your list details of people you find.
Particularly those who might be useful one day.

Read your local paper every day, even if you live in a major city.
Note anyone who should be on your list, whether you know them or not.
You'll have to do some detective work to find addresses.
Update your list as papers let you know when someone leaves your area.
Or they just help you add missing pieces to your jigsaw puzzle.

The best way to update is by phone.
Ring and say you're updating your list, is it OK to check some information?
Most people do not mind as you are not asking them to buy anything.

Now days the most important piece of information is an e-mail address.
They change regularly, so you need traditional contact information too.

A reason for calling people is to ask do they mind being on your list?
This is a legal requirement so you have to do it.
Seek permission over the phone, gather missing pieces at the same time.

Eventually you cull your list as you know the right people from others.
That takes time so it's all to start with.

2. At the beginning of a career an artist has many things to do.

It's not easy to work out what to do first and artistic stuff takes priority.
But professional artists sell artworks to people who want to buy.
Clients and prospective clients make it possible for a professional career.

It doesn't matter how well you work someone must buy.
There has to be a list of people so they can be contacted about what you do.
Otherwise they are simply unaware of you and your work.
The main asset you need in your career is a list of prospects and clients.
Having your own contact list is a first step towards managing your art career.
So it makes sense to start just as soon as possible.

A few people interested in your work is better than no list.
Start a list when you receive a first positive enquiry and build from there.

A contact list frees you from reliance on other people.
Not all in the art world is reliable so your own list can supplement them.
You'll increase the probability of success (for you and them).
You can also act independently when that is necessary.

Eventually a list means you initiate promotions that generate money.
It is like having a license to print money.
Well not quite a press "Send" and money arrives process but almost.
Whether you're doing your own promotions or not, you need a list.
It's the ultimate security and profit point in your career.

Perhaps you already have a small list?
Then as you make sales and establish interest build your list some more.
You could set up a contact list on your computer.
Ideally you'll be able to use CRM (client relationship management) software.
But it should not be too difficult to develop your own contact database.
And a database of works you've done, where they are and what they sold for.

Correct details is the most important step in creating a contact list.
Everything should be reviewed and edited before entering.

It's tedious, but not as frustrating as correcting errors already entered.
Particularly when they have been repeated multiple-times!
Care taken at the design stage reduces time and need for later editing.

The main way to keep your list accurate is to use it regularly.
The more a contact list is used, the more accurate it will become.
Address changes and other information can be regularly updated.
So send out notes, greetings, and such like material regularly.
Then you both maintain contact and also to keep the list up to date.
Update immediately new information arrives and you are always ready!

Keep your list simple.
The more complex the information collected, the more chance for errors.
There's no point collecting data if it isn't used either.

Retain data of any who haven't responded for a while but stop mailing.
The date of last purchase or response will provide a guide for this purpose.
Remove names of people who are really out of date.
Remove or put people into an 'off-list' who move with no forwarding address
People who ask to be taken off are definitely removed.

Can you identify people who are better clients than others?
Sometimes putting people or things in boxes can be useful, or necessary.
A caveman collects bones, stones and other objects for they like their looks.
Children collect things too which sometimes even survive into adulthood.
There are stamp, coin, doll, or teddy bear collections.

It's a natural human behaviour to collect objects and items of interest.
A way to make sense of things is put them in categories.
Dolls differ from bears, stamps and coins share value but are different too.
Your paintings are different from mine.

As we place things into broad groups we notice differences within.
Some bears are brown, but others white, some dolls are old, others new.
As knowledge and experience grows, so does the fineness of classification.

Putting people in boxes is really just this sort of activity.
We can't collect people, but we can still notice differences and similarities.
Then we can categorize them according to what we see.
As knowledge grows the boxes become more specialized and complex.

Real understanding of people is hard due to complexity and diversity.
BUT if their behaviour is broken into components it is easier.
Then we gradually put together a picture of the person, or group of people.
Putting people in boxes or categorizing knowledge about people is helpful.
It gives ways to use that knowledge and make complex things manageable.
We can study people from just a single point of view for example.
Categorize clients and prospects - do they all like everything you do?

Understand why people buy our art and we have information to use.
We might produce different works more likely bought by different groups.
Or we could market what we do to the people more likely to buy.
Perhaps we can do both - at least we now have some choice and direction.

3. If you know your target market create a hard to refuse offer!

A first step is create an opt-in strategy (people provide contact details).
Consider exactly which people you want to have in your contact list.
That's why you must know specifically who your opt-in strategy is aimed at.
Otherwise it is hard to run an opt-in campaign **AND** succeed in business too.
Knowing the client you seek, is critical to success in a career business.
There is no future dealing with wrong prospects - a waste of time and money!

You need hard information on your target contacts.
Then it's easier to have an opt-in offer that answers their specific needs.
You are starting to think about **WHAT** your target market really wants?

Time management is the key to career efficiency.
Many people, in all walks of life do not manage their time effectively.
Artists typically spend most of their art related time painting.
BUT a career will not happen if you do not give sufficient time to business.
Contacts made and maintained, promotions organized and attended to.
There are many essential tasks and plans - it's the same in any business.

Your plan assumes a successful and efficient list.
Your database should have many people who are genuine prospects.
Eventually just having a lot of people is not good enough.

But you can never be all things to all people.
Decide what strongly relates to your identity in a client's mind and stick to it.
Look for people attracted by that and be single-minded, as persistence pays.

Conduct regular client surveys so you know exactly who they are.
Know where they live, income level, education, and purchasing history.
Best prospects have these characteristics too so you know where they are.

Successful marketing is characterized by relentless, regular contact.
People need to be aware of your marketing message a number of times.
Only then will more than a few even think of responding.

Having a quality contact list makes this possible and manageable.
Develop systems to ensure that things you want to do always happen.
For example, you can check off the steps you need to follow-up after a sale.
There are other activity cycles you do often which also could use this way.
A quality contact list facilitates this kind of activity.

Persistence works.
No doubt you've heard the statement 'Faint heart never won a fair lady!'
Many sales people (not just artists) give up far too soon.
Each sales attempt can be different, but persist for five or six attempts.
Your contact list will allow you to track your activity in this regard.

Be religious following up contacts, if you say you'll do something, do it.
A phone call is all that's needed to find how the new painting looks on a wall.
That's why phone numbers should be in your contact list.

You compete with all kinds of things for a prospect's spare $.
You may think that you and your work are different from anything else.
BUT this is not necessarily what anyone else thinks.

You are not just in competition with other artists either.
Other ways their money is spent are a holiday, new curtains or mother dying.
So without a contact list, being truly competitive is just not possible.

4. Other ways to obtain and use names and addresses.

A first step in is obtain names and addresses of potential clients.
Privacy laws make passing on names to other parties difficult, even illegal.
So you have to develop your list by doing your own prospecting (research).

There are people who have NOT seen your work.
Such people are suspects, known to buy similar works to yours for example.
Those who are interested but haven't bought are prospects.

An electoral roll has information like first names and also occupation.
You can adopt a better approach than is the case without this knowledge.
You can get on first name terms for example.

When a client is a business, a slightly different approach is needed.
You are committed to saving money, increasing profit, or enhancing prestige.
Provide business reasons for a purchase and organize things so it happens.

Get names and addresses from special promotions for that purpose.
Set yourself up in a shopping centre with a few of your paintings.
Many people go past and some will be interested in what you do.

You could also get contact details by showing your art at a home show.
People supplying details are likely to be interested in art (kitchen cupboards).

Attend exhibitions you have work in to collect names and addresses.
Position yourself near your work and talk to anyone who shows interest.
Say you are the artist, ask questions, answer as few as possible (not easy).
Visitors fill a form with name, address, email address and telephone number.

Give a business card and ask them to contact you with the information.
You will then give details of other exhibitions that have your work on show.
But you still do not have their details until they decide to contact you.

Write on the back of a painting is a way to reach buyers and prospects.
Provide contact details and also staple two or three business cards there too.
Then your name and address is more accessible to prospects.

Take regular ads in your local or suburban newspaper.
Ask interested people to contact you so you can let them know its availability.
Re-word this according to your taste and the actual information you require.
This is not cheap and may not give great results, particularly if done once.
BUT it could lead to free promotion by the newspaper with better results.

I know an artist who ran his own exhibition (Canberra some years ago).
The sole purpose was making contact with prospective clients (and gallery).
It was the beginning of what has become an outstandingly successful career.
The artist was/is totally focused, and that's been important in his success.

5. Sorting your names and addresses.

When we hit a bull's eye (at darts), we hit our target dead centre.
Your marketing should have targets too - your clients and potential clients.
Where possible keep the names and addresses of your clients.
Often this is difficult for you didn't make the sale.
In this case the gallery, agent, or art show organization, is your client.
However try to make sure they've kept a list of their buyers of your work.
Most galleries do this routinely, but art show organizers may or may not.

What if the organization does not keep buyer information?
Perhaps they could supply the names and addresses for you - at least ask.
It important to list people interested in buying your work even if not yet.
They are more difficult to identify, but most come in casual conversations.
Make sure you get name and address before the conversation is forgotten.

You've a list updated regularly of buyers or those interested in buying.
You, or the gallery, can then contact these people whenever you wish.
You can tell them about the new print that will be available shortly.

A qualified mailing list is the best thing for a successful exhibition.
If no-one comes it will not matter what the works are like!
A qualified list just means it was sorted and appropriate for its intended use.
A list of picture framers is not likely to be much help for sales at an exhibition.

Are your prospects the same as your clients?
But if you want them to be different, you must know in what way (wealthier).
Also do different things to what you're doing now, to attract new people.

6. As knowledge about prospects grow segment your list.

Start by writing down your specific target market say tourists.
List characteristics: travel, have time and money to spend, out of town, etc.
Probably you have several target markets, so segment them.
Well, who are your prospective clients?
Where do they live?
How old are they?
Are they male or female?
What sort of lifestyle do they lead?
What sort of jobs do they have?
Are they passing through or local?
What disposable income do they have?

Many prospects have a similar cluster of characteristics.
You can communicate with groups with greater precision if you know them.
Enjoy increased conversion rates and profits if you segment your list.
Segment is people into categories (or segments) with shared characteristics.
A segment if they've bought and another for if they say they will (but haven't).

There are many ways to segment potential (or even actual) clients.
Then it is possible to send different things to different groups on your list.
For example on the how they prefer to be contacted (mail, phone, email).

Once it is segmented your contact list starts to become really useful.
The more you use it the better it becomes.
This is because you stay "top of mind", so when they think art they think you.
You increase chances of contacting as they think of buying or decorating.

Keep the list up-to-date.
Identify those who don't live at an address or whose email is invalid.
Then your list works better, and at the same time, is more economic?

Divide prospects and clients into smaller, more focused groups like:

Which products did they buy (watercolour, oil, landscape, art class)?
How frequently do they buy (every few months, on their anniversary)?
When was their last purchase (last week, six months ago, three years back)?
How much do they pay for one your works (varies, usually around $5000)?
How do they typically buy (quickly, take their time, need persuasion)?
How do they usually pay (cash, pay-off, etc.)?
What are their specific interests (landscapes, portraits, equine, large works)?
Where do they live (this suburb, next city)?
What is their age group (over 30 with young kids, nearly retired)?
How long have they been in your list (new, many years, five years)?
Where did they come from originally (referred by, passing by, tourists)?

One article I've read lists nine levels of segmentation.
Geographic (people who live in your suburb or town).
Demographic (people who are doctors).
Geo-demographic (accountants living in your city).
Socio-economic (people whose incomes are over $100,000 per annum).
Usage (people who buy antique furniture).
Benefits / needs (people who want to keep up with their peers).
Expectations (people who have indicated an interest in your work in the past)
Psychographic values (people who love what you paint)
Value to you / lifetime value (best spending and most recent clients).

Segmentation by values has become an increasingly useful method.
Values are emotional and usually strong.
Understanding core values allows you to integrate with your prospects.
Then they differentiate you from other artists.
It's possible to develop a relationship with clients on this basis.

There has been much written about the lifetime value of a client.
A lower cost of retention relative to finding and converting new clients.
But do not waste time and money on people who just want to have a chat.

Audit the economic value of differing client segments.

Then target those with high economic value to you.

This analysis identifies, by client segment, what their value is to you.

Also how they see you versus opposition and what they require to stay loyal.

As a professional artist you do need to make money.

Follow this strategy for guaranteed to see better results with your promotions.

So start segmenting your list, and get a definite edge on your competitors.

Here's how you can put this proven technique to work for your career:

Sort your current contact list into highly focused segments.

This could be clients who have purchased works from you before.

Also prospects who haven't purchased, new clients, or other segments.

Base segments on information you have on your existing contact list.

Then create different promotions for each segment of your list.

Target with highly personalized messages that speak to wants and needs.

Continue over the years necessary for the long-term value to be realized.

2. Why a contact list?

Reviewed by Mike O'Hagan – (Hong Kong, China.)

1. Why isn't a passion for art enough?
2. Many artists believe they do not need a contact list at all!

1. Why isn't a passion for art enough?

Some readers will know the Ford Motor Company once owned Jaguar.
Like many manufacturers, Jaguar was losing money, Ford was the rescuer.
The following story was in a motor industry magazine.

Jaguar was run by people who cared more about Jaguar than anything.
They had great cars but were losing money!
'When Ford brought process to that passion, you've got a lethal combination.
You've got both sides of the brain.' (Mike Dale Chairman Jaguar USA)

Like Jaguar, most artists have passion.
No doubt you are passionate about your art.
And if not then you should be for that's what drives you and keeps you going.
It's usually the other part, where problems arise.
It's the combination of career skills with passion that is lethal.
It makes scarce resources work effectively, whatever the amount available.
Do you have the systems to put your passion, skills and talent to work?

Let's say you do indeed have the passion.
The following could trigger that needed combination of process and skills.
They could help break through barriers to attain the career of your dreams.
One of the most important career processes is your contact list!
So just how well do you have things organized?
Do you waste time, money, talent, opportunity or scarce resource?

It's easy to adopt an image which changes depending on the situation.
Some people act one way with their employees and another with a superior.
Then in an entirely different way with people who unconnected with work.

To behave appropriately we modify behaviour according to context
The behaviour we show in a church is different from Sunday football.

Sales people are often trained to adjust their behaviour.
It changes according to characteristics displayed by a prospective client.
Actors and actresses are able to mimic a range of different people.

BUT one's real self, our true nature if you like, is constant.
We don't change according to the environment but always the same person.
Different environments highlight different facets of our character.

When there is a continuing business situation.
Sooner or later, you and the people you deal with, show their real persona.
This happens, even the previously mentioned trained sales people or actors.
It also happens for the people we deal with too.

Ego also has a considerable impact in business.
Understand this and you're in a position like Sir Humphrey in 'Yes Minister'.
Information gained from the egotist can be used to your own advantage.
We tend to forget that business is a constant process of keeping a guard up.
At the same time encouraging others to drop theirs.

But you must actually meet someone in person.
Otherwise none of that matters and that's where a contact list is essential.
We can stay in touch and arrange meetings with people.

2. Many artists believe they do not need a contact list at all!

People who sell need the contacts for the artist's concern is to paint.
But what happens if sales fall away, or are in insufficient numbers?
Whatever it is, it is **NOT** that your works are not 'good enough'!

The most likely reason is that the wrong people are being contacted.
Your artistic future (money & fame) depends on the right people buying.
It also depends on building sales momentum from that point.

The right contact list is the beginning of your recovery.
You can be pro-active generating an income stream if you know what to do.
Then there's a different mind-set.
How you develop a contact list is an extension of this thinking.
You need people to sell to, so where are the best prospects?

The best source of new prospects is old clients.
They mainly arrive by what is commonly termed 'word of mouth' advertising.
Can you harness this powerful force?
People who have bought in the past are the most likely to buy again!
Their friends and associates are the next likely group of potential buyers.
If you have a contact list you can reach them.

Now you should understand the main purpose of a contact list.
As the name implies a contact list allows you to contact people on that list.
These days a contact list is more often a list of email addresses.
Any gallery will have a list of buyers and prospective buyers.
Usually they will not supply you with those names, not even of your work.
But why waste your time doing the gallery's job anyway?
Well you are just beginning a professional career if you read this.
So it is very unlikely you have a gallery at this stage.

Approaching a gallery you should do further down the track.
Your career foundation is preparing for that step.
You are preparing so it will be successful for you **AND** the gallery.

That's why you need to develop a contact list.
Then you'll have a better understanding of what the gallery actually does.
You'll also have a bargaining chip in negotiations with prospective galleries.
You can supply them with your contact list!

Use your contact list for:
Acquisition:
Get NEW clients for your work.
Your present database won't do this if it only contains past buyers.
By building your list, you reach out to new people.

Retention:
To keep the clients you have.
Keep contacting so they don't go elsewhere, they might if they forget you.
Regular contact is necessary.

Motivation:
Fire your clients so they buy more of your works (eventually at an exhibition).
You can also cross-sell or up-sell to suitably targeted contacts.
Cross-sell is to sell products or services related to the original purchase.
Up-sell to sell more expensive or larger quantities than an original purchase.

Reactivation:
Lapsed clients can be reactivated so don't write anyone off.
They may be saving, just received a windfall or otherwise ready to buy.
You can nudge them in your direction.
So when should you follow up with your clients?
The best time to offer backend products is at a natural follow up opportunity.

Follow up after a purchase:
Right after someone buys send a thank you with an offer of a related product.
Offer clients insurance on artworks with a company that has a spotter's fee.
If you hold art classes offer students a special deal on supplies they'll need.

Follow up on a purchase anniversary:
An easy way to get a follow-up promotion in front of your clients.
Send an offer one month, six months, or a year after a first purchase.
Email them to ask how they're enjoying the painting.
Let them know you've more at a special discount price for previous clients.

Follow up whenever you can provide new products or information:
If you sell art supplies and you've just received new watercolour paper.
Contact clients who bought watercolour or acrylic paint, sell paper at a price.
There's a good chance they'd be interested in a quality paper.

BUT backend products HAVE to be what your market is interested in.
If you segment your list properly that should not be difficult to do.

3. Using your contacts.

Reviewed by Martine Norman - (Essex, United Kingdom)

1. Do you actually keep in touch?

2. Get your contact list right and open the door to opportunity.

3. I assume you are interested in making money as an artist.

4. Can you turn every client into a satisfied one?

5. Who is your client?

1. Do you actually keep in touch?

When you first left the family nest, did your mother want you to write?
Those readers who are a more mature in years would have such memories.
More recently mothers have said to their offspring, don't forget to call.

This is not just important for children, it's also important for artists.
I've mentioned contact lists and their importance are for professional artists.
Well it's not much use having a great list of addresses unless they're used.
That's really the point of the exercise - addresses let you contact people.

The people you should keep in touch with are clients and prospects.
How you do this depends on your particular approach to selling your work.
For beginning professionals this is usually direct to the buyer.
People come into your studio, home or gallery and purchase works from you.
You have their name, address and phone number and email address?

You can send them invitations next time you have an exhibition.
But at this stage of your career that is still a long way down the track.
Even then it's a bit like giving mum a ring on Mother's Day or her birthday.
Actually it's more like giving her a ring when it's your birthday or Christmas.
It's not very subtle, and from her point of view nowhere near often enough.

Mum would like you to call her every week, or at least once a month.
She wants to continue being part of your life and sharing it with you.
They don't know you as well as mum, but they'd like to know you better.

But they bought a painting, and so are part of your artistic life.
They may want to develop that further.

They want to know what you are doing, what your plans are and so on.
Obviously you won't have the time to contact them as often as they'd like.
BUT you can at least maintain a regular routine of keeping in touch.

It also makes sense to continually re-sell to your prospect base.
Keeping in touch regularly allows you to do this.
Continually advance reasons why they should buy or promote your work.

Now this is just a little different from giving mum a ring.
It's like ringing and suggesting what you'd like for your birthday or Christmas.

Be direct or quite subtle depending on the nature of your relationship.
The call, letter, or email to the client is a sales call.
The intention is to develop more sales from existing clients and prospects.

Most sales professionals regularly phone write and visit their clients.
This includes real estate people, car salesmen, insurance agents and others.
They're not social contacts but how they go about their job.
It's what the best galleries also do!

This contact should be planned and regular.
Write, fax, phone, email or call on a regular basis.
Variations might vary from a short hand written note to full scale sales letters.
You might set aside a Monday a month to give priority to phoning buyers.
On the other hand you could phone one or two clients each night.
It depends on whether you have home phone numbers or work related ones.
Home is best so start with best clients and gradually go to the just interested.

No sales = no money = no career.

2. Get your contact list right and open the door to opportunity.

We can learn from other people who operate in this field.
Factors that determine success or otherwise of a promotional campaign.
List of people contacted, offer, creative aspect and headline are the best.

Of them a contact list, or people mailed to, is by far the most important.
Basically, if you don't reach the right people, then nothing else matters.
Reach the right people, but don't attract attention (headline) nothing matters.
If an offer (what's for sale, price) doesn't appeal how it's done doesn't matter.

Many artists and galleries spend their time on the creative area.
They give little thought to the other aspects of a direct marketing campaign.
This is probably fairly natural and also enjoyable.

But the right list is the most important!
Names and addresses of those interested in buying or have bought.
It actually doesn't matter where they live.
Often people who live a long way from a gallery, know interested locals.
Sometimes they even buy over the phone!
So collect names and addresses all the time.
It doesn't matter if you haven't every little detail, just start!

Supply your list to each gallery you show at before any of exhibition.
Don't worry if they use your names for other artists.
When this happens you can be sure they'll be using other artist's lists for you.
All artists benefit from this type of activity, although it costs a gallery more.

A gallery should build a list of buyers and likely buyers of your work.
Just as you have and are doing.
The core may be the same as yours, but they have other names too.
Initially their list is small and that's why they need to use other artist's lists.
They should also make a few guesses of possible buyers.

This list is not very effective, but that's how you (and gallery) start.
More people should be added to your list as they see work in the gallery.
Friends of previous buyers can be added as well.

List building takes time.
That's why you should stick with a gallery long enough for them to do this.
Exhibit at a gallery where the other works are normally something like yours.
Then people on the gallery's list are more likely to like your work too.
The list building is quicker than for an orphan artist that takes a long time.

3. I assume you are interested in making money as an artist.

BUT there is NO need to compromise your SINCERITY and INTEGRITY!
Paint because there's something you want to paint, or an idea you want to
develop, or something you want to try, or for anything intrinsic to the work
and your experience.
Any other reason and it will be hard to maintain motivation and enthusiasm.
Particularly in the long term (as a career should be).

A professional artist is a self-employed business person.
You pay out money in advance of earning it.
Initially you learn what you need to do before you can get a financial result.

Re-selling to previous buyers can be a very smart thing to do.
Research has shown that a person buying three times is likely to buy more.
It may pay to offer an incentive for those who made a purchase from you.
Offer a discount, or add-on or incentive price at an exhibition.
Bundle products or whatever necessary for second and third purchases.
You basically need to breed collectors of your works!

Price so people buy more expensive works than originally intended.
Only have a limited number of smaller, cheaper works (or none at all).

This strategy worked for an artist who was left out cheaper works.
He probably sold fewer works than may have otherwise been the case.
But the dollar return was considerably better than he had anticipated.
People who wanted to buy had to go up a notch more than they intended.

Could you add dollars by cross-selling sketches linked to the works?
Have reports and articles on how you work, your philosophy, or subjects.
Anything else you think people would want to know.
CD's of you at work, or related to the works being sold, is another avenue.
Greeting cards and prints can be cross-selling devices add $ to your income.

Find ways to give early supporters a chance to profit in a big way.
If you can do this you'll have word of mouth working overtime on your behalf.
It's one of the reasons why it's not a bad idea to sell works cheaply, at first!
If there are many sales, later move prices up and first buyers are rewarded.
Make sure that they know this so they'll be able to tell other people.
They will then buy at the current prices before they go up again!

Is there any advantage in repetition?
Regular promotions (Easter, Christmas, end of financial year, Mother's Day).
People associate the events and look for your promotion before you start.

Can your marketing get cheaper?
Most marketing, particularly advertising has a high initial cost.
In time this reduces as you get to know what works and what doesn't.
Measure your marketing results to provide this information.
Set up your measuring devices before you actually do the marketing.
It's usually too late to measure (before and after effect) if you don't!

4. Can you turn every client into a satisfied one?

How could you make every one of your clients a satisfied one?
Make them so contented they return again and again and buy regularly,
AND they'll send new clients your way too?

There are proven ways to do this, which include:
Reducing the risk for your clients.
Going the extra mile.
Providing exceptional after-sales service.
Personalizing your offers.
Listening to your clients.

Customer service means the client is number ONE.
That applies across all business (online, offline, retail, service, hospitality).
Your art business is absolutely no different.

Provide better service than expected clients will keep coming back.
It's good business sense to go an extra mile and add value to their purchase.
There is a cost up front but a payoff is more referrals and repeat business.
Sometimes when an extra service costs nothing, what does a smile cost?

Another example is you give copyright away with each painting.
If you earn nothing from copyright now then there is no cost to you.
But it is a valuable extra for your client.

If your customer service is really good you might even charge more!
You know your clients are willing to pay extra for those services you provide.
At the very least you could test this idea.

List all the extra services you provide to your clients (or could provide).
Make sure your clients know about them too.
A service they don't know about is no service at all.

Here are some possibilities:
Free delivery and hanging.
Arrange framing according to client preference.
Provide a free annual valuation.
Provide a sturdy carry-bag, with your logo, to take the new work home in.
Give away copyright (although selling it is better).

Like most people your clients are probably busy.
Although it may not seem so when they visit you.
Do anything to make their lives easier and it will be appreciated.
And also worth paying more for.
So as well as a painting, provide greater convenience.

For example you could advertise some extra services, but not others.
New clients could be surprised by a little extra bonus they didn't know about.
Perhaps six of your greeting cards with their purchase - that's worth doing.
A few dollars for a new client, worth hundreds or thousands in lifetime value.
Becomes a delighted new client and the mathematics make sense!

Provide excellent after sales support and you'll over-deliver.
Businesses make a basic mistake thinking a job is done after a first sale.
Artists and galleries make this mistake too.
A quick after sales email or phone call to check that everything is OK.
That can really be appreciated by clients, old and new.

Relieve "buyer remorse" by reinforcing positive feelings.
That's about you and your art business.
Remind your new client that merely because their work is new.
It has a prominence that eventually will assume a more normal perspective.

Check with clients and find out how they use your work (where hung).
And what they really like and dislike about it.
So you can refine what you do (maybe) and your marketing (probably).
You can also head off any problems before they become complains.

How can you build a more personal relationship with your clients?
Listen to their concerns and act on them.
Most clients are reasonable.
They know things go wrong and people make mistakes.
Even sometimes things happen that were simply unavoidable.

But they still like you to acknowledge that you've made a mistake.
And to know that you'll do your best to prevent it from happening again.
That's why good restaurants give you a free bottle of wine if you meal is late.
Provide a free dessert if they get an order wrong.
Or replace a poorly prepared dish with no questions asked.

Making clients happy makes your job easier and more profitable.
Are you a professional artist?
Without clients this isn't possible so what are you doing to keep them happy?

5. Who is your client?

A client is the proper client for your artworks or artistic services.
Whatever proper means, not everyone with money will meet this criteria.

So are some clients more important than others?
I remember the first painting I bought was from an artist friend's exhibition.
He put the exhibition on himself so we went to offer support as 'artist friends'.
We had no intention of buying but decided to buy a work we particularly liked.
We paid a small deposit and went on our way.

Shortly after a capital city art gallery proprietor visited the exhibition.
She wanted to buy 'our' painting.
But our artist friend had made a deal and couldn't sell the work again.

From an artist's career viewpoint who was the proper client?
Was it us, just two friends, or the important gallery owner?

The reason for the exhibition was to attract this gallery owner.
It was a strategy to become a part of her team of artists.
There is no question the artist would prefer to sell to the gallery owner.
She was the proper client.

We have found out since, the artist's wife really liked this painting too.
It was only in the exhibition so the gallery owner saw his best work.
Fortunately this turned out well and he did become one of the gallery artists.
Our painting was on the cover of a retrospective catalogue a few years ago.
But it could have been different - and we still have the painting!

This story also illustrates the professionalism of our artist friend.
He knew who the proper client was.
This knowledge had guided all of his thinking, except when selling to us.
Even then he couldn't know that her response to the work would be similar.

How can we avoid the problem my friend had?
How can we make sure the right people buy our works?
We need to test potential clients (prospects) so they are proper clients.

Sales people can do this by asking questions and so can you.
Test all aspects related to your concept of a proper client.
What sort of work do they own now and what are they looking for?
What styles do they like?

Do their answers match your ideal client?
But also ask where do they live?
Do they entertain frequently?
Where are they likely to hang your work?

Ask questions and look for answers that lead to profitable outcomes.
A gallery owner can sell many of your works, so they are profitable.
Leaders in a social or professional group are likely to generate many sales.
Wealthy people can buy more than those on more modest incomes.
That's not just because they have more to spend!
They also have more wall space and even several houses or offices.

We should ask questions to determine if a prospect is a proper client.
We should also test our artworks and services so they are for such a client.
For instance the price should be right - not too high, but not too low either.
How do you test this?
Phone past clients and ask their opinion; particularly those like proper clients.

What if you have a work the National Gallery might want?
Do you sell to someone without making an effort to sell to the gallery first?
How about a sale to your local council?
What about where the work is displayed publicly and many people see it?
All of these are important potential sales.

If you identify a proper client how do you avoid my friend's mistake?
Offer a preview of your work **BEFORE** anyone else has a chance to buy.

Write down exactly what sort of clients you would like to have.

Now develop a range of questions to test if prospects match your ideal.
You can also segment your contact list to reflect your discoveries.

4. Keeping contacts.

Reviewed by Hilarie Couture - (Vancouver, Canada)

1. It is easier to rekindle old relationships than start new ones.
2. Computers are magic for managing a database.
3. Does your database make money?
4. What you need to know to effectively manage contacts.

1. It is easier to rekindle old relationships than start new ones.

You only need to make contact about 4 times a year.
Yes, it's that simple, although more frequently is even better.
But you do need a contact list and then your client base is a gold mine!
Sales to existing clients increases revenue by 30% to 50% due to lower cost.
That's why it's important to follow up with everyone who purchases from you!

So how do you reach your existing client base?
One excellent follow-up strategy is **AUTOMATED SEQUENTIAL OFFERS**.
The aim is to draw buyers back to your studio, website, or gallery.

E-mail clients after an initial sale to thank them for the purchase.
Ask if they have any questions and also offer a related product.
This isn't hard because you know what they bought initially.

Another strategy is e-mail new offers and special promotions.
Target your e-mail communications to clients based on their sales history.

For example, send a special promotion to all your first-time clients.
Or, you might send a "thank you" promotion to your long-term repeat clients.
In each e-mail, offer a product or service related to the initial sale.

Not sure what you can offer as a backend item (the offer)?
Offer a related product they're likely to be interested in (hanging materials).
Offer more of the same product (another painting of a similar size and price).
Offer an upgrade to the initial product (a new and more expensive frame).

Even more backend offers.
Offer a service that assists with the use of the product (a free valuation).
Offer a service to apply to the product for them (the copyright).
Offer information to improve the use of their product (a biography for friends).
Offer other people's products for a commission (you think of this one).

Time your offers for maximum success.
Send out your follow-up offers 3, 7, and 10 days after the initial purchase.
These are when new clients are most likely to make a **SECOND** purchase.

The start point in direct marketing is decide what you want to get.
Later you measure against this to see if you've been successful or not.

Direct mail works and can help you:
Find new clients
Retain current clients
Upgrade and cross sell to current clients
Prospect cost effectively for new clients
Build your identity over the long term
Enhance the work your gallery does
Win back lost clients

Try to be as specific as possible about what you want to achieve.
The above seven points provide a starting point to develop your thinking.
Find more clients in the same suburb that most of your present clients live in.
Contact your present clients more regularly.
Suggest additional purchases to your present clients.
Support the exhibition invitation your gallery is sending out for you.
Provide past clients with a special incentive to buy again.

You might even be more specific.
Introduce your new watercolours.
Generate sales leads which you can follow up.
Maybe you'd like people to actually come to your studio?

You must decide something or you'll do nothing at all.

If promotions are quantified, it's easy to measure success or lack of.
I want to sell ten works.
I want 50 people to attend.
The numbers can be compared with the actual sales or people who came.
In time your predictions will become more accurate.

From these different objectives you need different items to email.
Probably there will be different people to email to as well.
Other forms of communication might be used in conjunction or separately.
Your objectives provide a focus for all aspects of every phase of a campaign.
So objectives should be clear, realistic, quantified and related to a time.

Once you've decided what you want to achieve study what you sell.
Ask yourself, what you have to offer a prospective buyer.
What will they gain by acquiring one of your works?
What is going to appeal to a potential client, see your work as a client does?
If you are not sure how they see your works, then ask some prospects.

Basically most people are interested in 'What's In It For Me' (WIIFM).
Well, what benefit does owning one (or more) of your works offer the client?
Is it improved lifestyle, prestige, save time, save money, or one-up on Jones?
Trying to work this out is not easy, so here's a way you can tackle the task.

Find a client benefit flowing from features of you or your work.
Try to be specific about the benefits for example, you paint historical themes.
A benefit for the client could be your paintings evoke feelings of nostalgia.

Benefits will usually relate to feelings.
It's more important to promote them than to describe your works.
Common error in artist promotion but to do anything you need a contact list!

2. Computers are magic for managing a database.

A contact list is like an address book except it is electronic.
Usually this information doesn't change and a base for marketing database.

Comprises files about clients or potential clients and includes:
'Title' (Mr. Mrs. Ms. Miss Dr Prof. Rev etc.)
'Name' (first and family or last names)
'Postal address' (include zip code)
'Phone numbers'
'Email address'
'Promotion source' (how did they arrive as clients)

Your business file is similar to the contact file.
Enter position in company, location, company name and business details.

But you also need dynamic information which is data that changes:
Purchases in categories such as landscapes, small works, prints, etc.
Whether people are cash, credit buyers, or what?
Who spends the most money?
Which clients have bought the most?
How many works do they have?
What is their average price?
How long has it been between purchases?

The changing data makes a database profitable.
It turns a static database into a valuable marketing tool.

Most marketers enter answers to these questions under the headings:
Recency: When did they buy last?
Frequency: How often do they spend?
Monetary value: How much do they spend?
This allows you to see exactly who is supporting your art career.
You'll be able to reward best clients and identify those who need more work

Your marketing can now be something more than mere guesswork.
Code responses to find out about promotions and media with best results.
Other promotions could lead to different results, but all can be compared.
From that point you can spend money where the best result is most likely.

You'll know how to:
Segment your market (categorize your clients according to buying patterns).
Customize products and services to your client's interests.
Target your marketing efforts more finely.
Target increased purchases per client.
Encourage larger purchases per client.

3. Does your database make money?

An efficient database can help you earn money from your art career.
Is yours as efficient as it could be or what else do you want it to do?
Otherwise how do you know if you have an efficient database or not?

What kinds of questions should it answer?
If you are going to use that data it has to answer some important questions.
What does this person like to be called?
Can you contact them by email?
Have they bought any of your artworks before?
These are a few questions your database should be able to answer.

What types of statistical analysis should it be able to do?
You should be able to do some for that is an advantage of a database.
How many people have bought your works?
What was the average price?
What is the average number of works owned per person?
What is the turn-around time for different aspects?
How often will you contact someone?
How often have you?
You don't want people slipping through the cracks.

Your database should help you maintain critical time deadlines.
How up to date must the data be for different aspects?
Right up to date is the correct answer.
But how do you do this?
Can this task be automated which is the best way.

What data is needed to allow required functions to be performed?
You need email address data as a minimum.
Without email addresses you simply cannot contact people that way.
Do not collect or record information you will not use (date of birth perhaps).

These days there are a number of contact programs that can be bought.
The problem is you will not need all the possibilities that they make available.
Start with minimum information and gradually add to that as the need arises.

How should you update or replace data?
Some elements will need updating or replacing regularly.
If this can be automated then a great deal of time is saved.
Decide intervals between updating or replacing data (week, month, annual).

What data is important and what isn't?
You have to decide, but if it is unimportant then why keep it?
Will unimportant information be important in a year? Three? Five?
That's why!

What haven't I thought of?
There's bound to be something.
Don't worry because soon it will come to your attention then you deal with it.

4. What you need to know to effectively manage contacts.

They guarantee the highest possible response to any mail-out sent:
It's important to stay on top of your "subscribe" and "unsubscribe" requests.

Always treat requests to unsubscribe from your list seriously.
People not removed from a list after an unsubscribe request say you spam.
You can quickly find yourself in trouble with your ISP.
It's just as important people who ask to be added are subscribed right away.
You never know which subscription request will end up being a best client.

Handle automatically subscription and unsubscribe requests.
Otherwise you should take care of them just before you send out a mailing.
This means a list is as current as possible so you don't have to do this daily.

Before any mailings make sure you don't have duplicate addresses.
There are always some who opt in, leave, and come back a few days later.
Then they sign up again, forgetting that they've already joined.

Keeping a list clean is not just removing unsubscribes and duplicates.
Cleaning your list means sifting messages that "bounce back" after a mailing.
Deciding which ones should be removed from your list completely.
Also which ones you might want to try mailing again.

"Bounced" messages are messages not successfully delivered.
Most bounced messages are either "soft" bounces or "hard" bounces.
Soft bounces are messages that couldn't be delivered at the time sent.
They may be deliverable at some time in the future.
These types of bounces are usually caused by the recipient's full inbox.

Hard bounces are messages that can never be delivered.
Hard bounces usually caused by a wrong email address when opting in.
Or a subscriber no longer uses an email address they originally opted in with.
Occasionally you can figure out the correct email address and give that a try.

Generally hard bounces should be deleted immediately.
If you leave them in you'll go through unnecessary bounce messages.
That happens every time you send a mailing, a waste of your valuable time.
However it can be worth phoning these people to alert them of their situation.

If you continue emailing an invalid address you can be in real trouble.
This is one of the methods used to identify spammers.
Repeated messages to a "dead" address is a problem to the receiving ISP.
Emails returned as soft bounces should be dealt differently.
Soft bounces are a result of a temporary problem - like a full mailbox.
Re-send your promotions to all soft bounce addresses a couple of days later.

You'll be surprised how many messages get delivered on a second try.
Since you've already written the email, there's little extra work on your part.

Divide your list and gain more subscribers
Given the emails people receive these days, most only want what's relevant.
Unfair as it is anything irrelevant could be considered spam and reported.

People know a message you send is something they want they open it!
An effective way to market is email to different prospect base segments.
People who segment have better results than for undifferentiated mailings.
There are many ways to segment a list depending on information you have.

Email automation makes it not only possible, but simple!
Gain your recipients' attention by using their name.
Personalize the subject line.
The best technique to boost a response to emails than personalization.
It's a way of establishing trust and building rapport.

Someone's name makes them feel they have a relationship with you.
Nothing gets a person's attention faster than their own name!
Personalizing a subject line makes an email authentic and safe to open.
Recipients are more likely to view your email as from a trusted source.

Imagine typing individual names into the subject line of every email!
Grow your list to more than 50 or 100 people, it becomes unmanageable!
But there are many email marketing software packages available these days.
They will help you completely personalize your campaigns automatically.
Thus, saving a great deal of time and effort.
Such software is definitely a worthwhile investment.

Privacy legislation means a business database has to be used legally.
Be familiar with the laws and take them into account with a contact list.
The client's privacy must be respected.
The law is not against collecting this information; it's about who you give it to.
When seeking information use a phrase such as 'by the way.
Follow with a request (who else do you know, interested in work like mine).

There's no point in a storehouse of client information unless you use it.
But a basic principle is that people must be willing to be contacted.
First contact should mean recipient willingness to receive mail, emails or call.
Say you don't want to annoy anyone and will remove them from your list.

People who want to be taken off are removed.
Not just because of the legislation.
Further contact is a waste of money and liable to generate negativity as well.

The phone call can be more like a friendly chat.
The prospect never realizes you have a similar friendly chat with everyone.
The key is to develop a script for what you want to say and achieve.
The script needn't be read word for word, but should be key points covered.
Then you can develop your own style, personality and flavour.
You respond to the person on the other end of the phone.

Perhaps you are ringing all who have bought a work recently?
You want to find out if they are happy with it and do their friends like it?
Would any of friend be interested in attending your next exhibition?

Special offers can be made to specific groups too

They receive privileges such as a preferential purchase opportunity.
They could also receive early notification of any exhibition.
Mailings to this group should be considerably better than a general approach.

You might experiment with various forms of mailings.
Use a simple approach with special attention to key elements.
A personalized letter, a brochure or invitation about the offer are some ways.
There should be a way to reply, and a message on the envelope.

Test everything to make sure your results justify the expenditure.
Normal newspaper, radio or TV advertising can be used in conjunction.
Provided you control how it is linked with your mailings and telemarketing.
Don't forget the possibility of free publicity either.

Track the response to everything you do.
You'll know the success of your promotions, which means you can improve.
That's why it does pay to give quite a deal of thought to the response device.
Make it easy for people to do whatever it is you want them to do.
Also make it easy for you to keep track of every marketing initiative.
Your database is one of the most valuable resources your art business has.

From time to time your contact list should be modified.
A contact list should reflect what you do.
People may ask to be removed and so you do that.
Other people's emails bounce so you place those contacts in a special list.
Generally prospects should not be removed from a list unless they request it.
Of course there are always new contacts to add.
No doubt you are doing things to attract people to being on your list.

Contact that is regularly irregular is the way to go.
Vary each message and stay in touch for years without giving any offence.
If you haven't heard from someone for a long time doesn't mean never will.
Try new offers, do things a bit differently, and be creative in your contacts.

5. WRAPPING UP.

Reviewed by Eliza McInnes - (Sydney, Australia).

1. What is the long term value of your clients?

2. People's memories vary greatly.

3. Under-promise but over-deliver.

4. Your contact list allows you to focus on marketing.

5. What will the lifetime value of your contact list be?

1. What is the long term value of your clients?

Segmenting clients will allow you to see different patterns of behaviour.
One aspect you should have considered is the long term value of a client.
Who has spent most, how frequently and at what average price?
By thinking beyond a single sale is possible to project into the future.
It may also mean we can consider a single sale in a different light.

Say you segment clients and have been for a number of years.
In this case you should be able to calculate the average $value of a sale.
The $ spent by clients divided by number of sales in a specific period of time.
We'll call this amount $X.

Also calculate the average number of sales for a typical client.
The total sales divided by the number of clients over the time (say 4 years).
Let's call this Y.

The long term value of a typical client will be $X Y.
Perhaps the average sale for your work is $1450 ($X)?
The average number of sales is 7 per client (Y).
The long term value (4 years) of a typical client is then $10,150 ($X Y).
Obviously some clients will spend more than this and others less.

This is very useful information.
If necessary you can spend up to $3000 or a little more on acquiring a client.
You'll still make a profit in the long run.

Naturally you'll probably spend a lot less than this.

If you know the long term value of a client you may spend more than now.

It will pay off if your figures are accurate.

So you need to keep the necessary figures for a period of time.

The calculations become reasonably accurate guides but initially you guess.

Also calculate the value of a specific client over the same period.

Now you can identify clients who return above average and those who aren't.

Try to upgrade the latter group, and certainly nurture the former clients.

If you are successful then the averages will change, for the better.

Contact lists let you to maintain or develop relationships with clients.

That continues over the years necessary for long-term value to be realized.

2. People's memories vary greatly.

How much of what you, or a gallery, say to a client will they remember?
Can they remember enough to convince their spouse when they get home?
That one of your works is an essential purchase!
Or for long enough to repeat it to their business partner!

If they can't, then the chances of a sale diminish.
After a sales presentation a typical buyer remembers ¾ of what was said.
But a week later this had dropped to a little more than ¼.
This doesn't show whether the points remembered were the key ones or not.
They may have been or they may not.

After a presentation, clients expressed high probability they would buy.
A week later there were marked changes in client enthusiasm.
Relatively few were likely to buy.

Basically, none of this is too surprising.
It reinforces if you don't make a sale immediately it's unlikely to be made.
No problems if you are selling a low cost item, directly to a potential buyer.
But you are selling something where buying decisions typically take time!
A prospect needs to consult with others (wife, accountant, boss, partner,)!
In other words you want to make a major sale, as artwork is to most buyers.

Relying on people to remember all that was said is not be good enough.
Potential buyers need help to remember the main points to convey to others.
If they are also involved in the buying decision you may not get to meet them.
Obviously the selling strategy must be different than with the one-shot sale.

Most artists and many galleries use single meeting sales techniques.
To sell artwork (particularly expensive works) something different is needed.

Write down how to plan to sell a $10,000 painting to a business.
How will they remember key points if talking to other decision-makers?
Perhaps you could provide notes of the main points for someone else?

Most business focus on their interests and small business is more so.
However it's possible to approach the small business on a personal basis.
For its likely the business is basically the person who owns it.
Whatever works so individuals to see art as worth investing, will work here.
Similarly whatever fails will fail here as well.

So for smaller business you don't think about them as a business.
Think about them as people.
Try to see what sort of benefit they might obtain from your artwork.
How can the work help them achieve love, pleasure, status or whatever?

Major companies are actually no different, if you get to the right people.
The right people are the decision makers.
This is usually the 'boss', but in some situations there are other right people.
The purchasing officer, boss's secretary, wife, or office manager.
Any of them could be the right person for buying artwork.

In this situation the first task is to track down the right person.
Then approach them on much the same basis as for smaller businesses.
The scale of a large business may mean more money for artworks.
On the other hand they may look for the $ value in everything they do.

In essence you have to show any business, what's in it for them.
What do they gain by having one, or more, of your artworks?
If you suggest they'll gain a worthy investment.
This has to be demonstrated to the business.
Even then, the business will weigh this against other worthy investments.
This is what individual buyers do too.

In times when money is plentiful, people can have a range of choices.
As economic circumstances become more difficult, the options narrow.
No persuasion will sell an artwork to a business that has no money.
Even if it's a worthy investment for they are interested in survival.
You'll have to show them how your gallery's artworks can help them survive.

3. Under-promise but over-deliver.

The secret of client satisfaction is deliver more than they expect.
If your clients expect an unframed work and it arrives complete with frame.
You have 'over-delivered' and a client won't just be satisfied, but delighted.
A frame costs quite a deal, and there's a chance they prefer a different style.
Alternative a small sketch of the same subject as the painting, framed or not.

The more you can delight your clients, the happier they will be.
And the more they will come back for repeat doses.
These days, when sales are difficult, such strategies may even be essential.
Take advantage of opportunities missed by those unprepared.
Market share and client loyalty is gained during a down turn.
Tends to be longer lasting and stronger than those gained in boom times.

There will always be people with money!
In affluent times competitors do all sorts of things to make life difficult for you.
Avoid rash promises, hype creates suspicion particularly if reality is different.
It's better to promise little.

Just say or do enough to get a prospect to view the works.
Under-promising has a lot going for it.
In fact it's a strategy that sets up enhanced satisfaction by your clients.
How little do you need to promise someone so they buy one of your works?

You have to find the right words for the job!
Most readers of what you wrote take 10 seconds or less to decide.
That's the time you have to convince them.

The most important words are the ones in your headline!
Your headline is the first thing your readers see.
It needs to capture attention, spark curiosity and compel them to read further.
The headline words also have to do all this **FAST**.

Most readers (at your site or of stuff you wrote) want information.
But that doesn't necessarily mean you should provide information.
They want information in relation to a problem they are trying to solve.
Maybe they are curious about art in their area?
Perhaps they want contemporary coloured paintings for a rumpus room?
They could be trying to work out how to reframe a painting they've inherited?

You just don't know what the problem is they want to solve?
So you need to find out what their problem is and then relate to that.

Alternatively what sorts of problems does your art solve?
Demonstrate a clear and genuine understanding of their wants and needs.
Then they'll be far more interested in what you have to say.

You've described a problem, now you have to solve it.
You need to do this so that it creates a powerful image in a readers mind.
Whatever you do get them to imagine the end result.

Now you're more than halfway down the track to making a sale.
"How to …" and "Discover …" headlines help people imagine an end result.

They aren't interested in what your painting or service (class) is like.
But they **ARE** interested in what it will do for them, a benefit not description!
This isn't easy for an artist to do.

We don't usually think that way.
Any painting you do will do many different things for a variety of clients.
They imagine the nods, smiles and admiring glances their new painting gets.
Every time someone sees it on their wall.

The important question in your reader's mind is "What's in it for ME?"
Make sure you answer this question and avoid telling and describing.

Write directly to your readers.

Write those headlines as if you are talking to your best client.

They're someone you know very well so they are the focus of all you write.

Write in the same way that you speak is a key aspect of this.

Possibly you need to modify this to use the same language as your readers.

If your works appeal to leather clad bikers.

Do not write the same way as for a homebody who specializes in quilting.

If you clients say "dude" then so do you, but if they say "folks" "dude" is out.

Don't tell them how great your art is.

They picture how great their lives will be after your work is on their wall.

Make sure your words are genuine.

Make your headlines stand out so readers get meaning in a glance.

Limit yourself to one important idea per line.

Use simple formatting such as bold and italics.

Your headline can have a massive effect on your sales.

You should spend quite a deal of time on it.

Once you have written a few headlines, **TEST THEM**.

Play around with them and test again and see which works best.

Do this a few times to discover the one that works best.

It will be worth the effort.

4. Your contact list allows you to focus on marketing.

It's a planned, thoughtful exercise that started a long time ago.
Most artists do not have a plan, let alone a marketing plan.
Plan your marketing for at least 12 months ahead,
Otherwise how can you expect anything other than random results?

Marketing begins before the painting commences.
You are the key person in your business.
A professional artist decides what you do.
Potential clients are part of your decision process.

You need to sell yourself to create your career.
This is not easy for many artists, but it can be learned.
People in other careers do this so there's no reason for artists to be different.

Good marketers know it is an investment where return outweighs cost.
Good marketers' measure.

As the plan is developed, question each expense.
Particularly its appeal to your target market and the likely cost efficiency.
What people want is an extra, emotional bonus buying something they love.

Is it easy to buy what you sell?
Sometimes artists make it hard for people to buy.
There is a reluctance to buy, for barriers have been put in place by the artist.
A client must buy for the right reasons for example.
Do you want to be a professional artist or not?
Other professionals do not have a problem with money!

People are selfish, lazy, uninformed and impatient.
Start with that and you'll be pleasantly surprised at what you find.
But art for everyone rarely reaches anyone.

Best clients are worth far more than average ones so choose clients.
Sack the ones who hurt your ability to deliver the right story to the others.

How valuable are your clients?
The actual value of a client to your career is the $ they spend in a year.
Multiplied by the number of years they spend.
You can estimate based on your experience with other similar clients.

Obviously this is more than just a single sale.
So you need a long term plan to maximize each client's value to your career.
It's too important to leave to chance.

Build relationships with your clients.
Really get to know your clients.
Satisfied clients get you new business by referring friends and associates.
Marketing is about far more than just advertising.

What are your client's wants and needs?
Have them as a priority so do your market research, ask them!

People don't buy what they need, they buy what they want!
Marketing that works is marketing that people choose to notice.
One disappointed prospect is worth at least ten delighted ones.
But often we neglect the clients' values.
Like one up on the Jones', or I'm successful.

Reminding a prospect of a story they know and trust is powerful.

Good marketers tell a story.
Effective stories link to the world view of people who are listening or reading.
An authentic story is the best way to survive in a conversation-rich world.

Keep your ego under control.
For some artists this is very difficult, after the isolation of the studio.
They just love the public aspects of their career.

Avoid spending money on functions for existing and potential clients.
You want them spending money instead.

Marketing is how you answer a phone, write invoices or returns policy.
When you send, or even pay, monthly invoices, send buying suggestions.
Base these on purchase history (best guess) of the person to whom it is sent.
At least use it as a way to distribute good news about your career.

Anticipated, personal, relevant material is better than unsolicited junk.
Business-to-business marketing is just marketing to consumers.
Except they happen to have a company to pay for what they buy.
Marketing to government is much the same.

Resist investing in advertising so your name and works are prominent.
For career momentum an exhibition is to sell works not just show them.

Artists more than most should find ways to boost the bottom line.
Learn from the big stores.
Corporations rely heavily on point of sale displays, called merchandising.
They are visual methods of attracting customer attention and making sales.

If people can visit your studio, what is the first thing they see?
Is it what you want them to remember?
What is the last item?
Could it be something inexpensive so you at least obtain some money?

Some sponsorship is useful for small, specific events at local level.
Sponsorship offers marketing opportunities at reasonable cost.
You are also seen as supporting your local community.
To get support you must give it!

Target your sponsorship for best results.
Your clients do not come from every section of the community.
A school football team might make sense if the school also has an art show.

Don't forget public relations.
Here I refer to inexpensive ways to communicate with the general public.

Like speaking at functions, or being the focus of a newspaper article.
Artists have a great deal going for them in this area; so don't be shy about it!

Look for other people you can work with.
Expand your circle of influence to reach areas not accessible previously.
You also cut costs by sharing with others who may or may not be artists.

You should track results of any major promotion.
Then you'll be able to re-invest appropriately.

5. What will the lifetime value of your contact list be?

A return from a contact list increases efficiency of OTHER activity.
Initially you learn what to do **BUT** the sale of an extra painting recoups.

The amounts shown are hypothetical to illustrate financial factor:
Your initial investment plus some promotion = $250

Time	Income	Gross	Cost	Profit
1 yea…….$100		…..$100 - $250	…..$250	……$150 (loss)
2 years…..$200		…… $200 - $150	….$150	……$150 =$100 (loss)
3 years…..$350		……..$350 - $100	….$125	……$125 = $125
4 years…..$450		……..$450 +$125	….$100	- $100 = $475

OK these amounts may not be exactly what you will earn.
BUT they do provide an idea of the kind of thing that is possible.
They do not guarantee anyone will achieve the same or similar results.
In any business, results vary, and will be based on background, dedication,
motivation individual capacity, business experience, expertise, and desire.

Each sale will build on the one that went before.
At some point your prices will move past your present levels.
In the second year sales will be higher and in the third more again.

In future years your prices can increase dramatically!
Referrals increase the number of works you can sell too.

BUT there is no cost-free way to start selling!
AND your works must be sold to earn money.
A break-even promotion is satisfactory to start and can set up your future.

In the beginning you will need enough income to pay your costs.
Otherwise you need an independent income source.
You will also need to keep your spending under tight control!

When the time comes supply a gallery who represents you with a list.
From your point of view it doesn't matter who sells your work only they do.
Over time a gallery should be building a personal mailing list for your work.
The more you can add to this the more effective it becomes.

Usually artists only supply details of people living near that gallery.
This is logical enough, but fails to take into account the mobility of buyers.
Often people who live long distances from a gallery know interested locals.
Sometimes they even buy sight unseen.
A gallery who deals in local clientele is their privilege, but probably a mistake.
If you wish to limit a gallery to local clientele, try but it may cost you sales.

You and your gallery work as partners, you are a major shareholder.
It does not really matter where the people live so long as you sell your work.
You can let them have the addresses of your friends and relatives too.
However, make this a separate list if they are not likely buyers.

Past buyers are the most likely future buyers.
Their friends, relatives and associates are also likely to be future buyers.
Your client base will be expanded more widely with this approach.
Eventually your circle of clients can cover a state or nation.

W H E R E   N E X T :

BUT being a professional artist is NOW harder than it ever was.
There are other books that link with this book.
You might need one or more of them:

PRICE RIGHT - Then sell.
http://www.amazon.com/dp/B087S85HS8

PLANNING - Means success.
http://www.amazon.com/dp/B087SCD1NY

CAREER BASICS - Planning.
http://www.amazon.com/dp/B087SCJYX3

FIRST WEBSITE - Simple is best.
http://www.amazon.com/dp/B087SFZ6RD

SUCCESSFUL SELLING - Learn how.
http://www.amazon.com/dp/B087SHDKPN

FRAMING = helps sales
http://www.amazon.com/dp/B087SGS6MB

CHRISTMAS - Special approaches.
http://www.amazon.com/dp/B087SHDKPN

TAKE THE PLUNGE - become professional
http://www.amazon.com/dp/B087SFTD61

PRODUCTIVITY – the foundation
http://www.amazon.com/dp/B087S87HLD

COPYRIGHT - making money from copyright sales.
http://www.amazon.com/dp/B0892HWYTV

N O T N O W :

Perhaps one of these books could interest you then?

Write about your own memories.
http://www.amazon.com/dp/B087DWKPTP

A simple way to start developing creativity.
If you are a parent, teacher or someone who meets a group regularly?
http://www.amazon.com/dp/B088T1KFQZ

Here is how most people start becoming an artist!
http://www.amazon.com/dp/B088Y1DPL6

More of my memories.
http://www.amazon.com/dp/B088Y4RPL9

Start an art career but it's NOW is harder than it ever was.
http://www.amazon.com/dp/B088T7VJ76

SEND TO:

**Know anyone interested in chocolate recipes?
Then send them this link.**

http://www.amazon.com/dp/B088Y4RPL9

Know anyone interested in THIS book?

http://www.amazon.com/dp/B087SM58GJ

www.ingramcontent.com/pod-product-compliance
Lightning Source LLC
Chambersburg PA
CBHW051226250726
48655CB00006B/2615